ENGINEERED BY NATURE

Killer Plants

By Louise and
Richard Spilsbury

BELLWETHER MEDIA • MINNEAPOLIS, MN

Jump into the cockpit and take flight with **Pilot books**. Your journey will take you on high-energy adventures as you learn about all that is wild, weird, fascinating, and fun!

This edition first published in 2017 by Bellwether Media, Inc.

No part of this publication may be reproduced in whole or in part without written permission of the publisher. For information regarding permission, write to Bellwether Media, Inc., Attention: Permissions Department, 5357 Penn Avenue South, Minneapolis, MN 55419.

Library of Congress Cataloging-in-Publication Data

Names: Spilsbury, Louise, author. | Spilsbury, Richard, 1963- author.
Title: Killer Plants / by Louise and Richard Spilsbury.
Other titles: Pilot (Bellwether Media)
Description: Minneapolis, MN : Bellwether Media, Inc., 2017. | Series: Pilot. Engineered by Nature | Audience: Ages 7-13. | Audience: Grades 3 to 8. | Includes bibliographical references and index.
Identifiers: LCCN 2016033341 (print) | LCCN 2016034171 (ebook) | ISBN 9781626175907 (hardcover : alk. paper) | ISBN 9781681033204 (ebook)
Subjects: LCSH: Carnivorous plants–Juvenile literature. | Dangerous plants–Juvenile literature.
Classification: LCC QK917 .S65 2017 (print) | LCC QK917 (ebook) | DDC 583/.75-dc23
LC record available at https://lccn.loc.gov/2016033341

Text copyright © 2017 by Bellwether Media, Inc. PILOT and associated logos are trademarks and/or registered trademarks of Bellwether Media, Inc. SCHOLASTIC, CHILDREN'S PRESS, and associated logos are trademarks and/or registered trademarks of Scholastic Inc.

Printed in the United States of America, North Mankato, MN.

Table of Contents

When Plants Attack	4
Venus Flytrap	6
Pitcher Plant	8
Sundew	10
Bladderwort	12
Corkscrew Plant	14
Dodder	16
Strangler Fig	18
Puya	20
Angel's Trumpet	22
Manchineel Tree	24
Doll's Eyes	26
Engineered to Survive	28
Glossary	30
To Learn More	31
Index	32

When Plants Attack

Plants are **engineered** by nature to survive in their environments. They **adapt** to get the food and space they need to grow. Some **species** also have special defenses to keep hungry animals away.

FAST FACT

Water hemlock looks innocent, but its poison can kill a victim in just 15 minutes.

Most plants make their own food from sunlight and air. This process is called **photosynthesis**. Some plants trap insects or other animals to get extra food. Others steal **nutrients** from other plants. These killer plants strangle, stab, or even **poison** their victims!

DID YOU KNOW?

Water hemlock is the most poisonous plant in North America. A small amount is enough to kill a cow, or even a human!

Venus Flytrap

A Venus flytrap opens its leaves wide to trap **prey**. Its sweet-smelling **nectar** attracts a fly.

The insect lands on the leaf, bending its short, stiff hairs. Snap! The leaf slams shut. Spikes around its edges lock together. They keep the fly from escaping.

The trap closes tightly. It squashes the fly. The plant releases special substances that break down the body into tiny pieces. Then the plant **digests** its victim.

DID YOU KNOW?

Venus flytraps grow in soils that are low in nutrients. They catch insects to get nutrients they need to survive. Some even capture small frogs!

FAST FACT

If a fallen leaf causes the trap to close, the plant opens to let the wind blow the leaf away.

ACTIVITY

Engineering in Practice

The spikes on a Venus flytrap form a cage. See how this works using your own two hands!

- Rest your hands on a table and place your palms and fingers together.
- Pull your palms apart (still resting on the table at the wrist).
- Spread your paired fingers out so there are gaps between them.
- Lace your fingers together and fold them over.
- Now you have made a flytrap!

Pitcher Plant

A pitcher plant looks like a jug with a wide bottom. It **lures** insects into its deadly trap. They come to feast on its sugary nectar. Instead, they get a nasty surprise.

Inside the pitcher, insects slide down its waxy, slippery walls. They fall into a pool of deadly liquid at the bottom. This liquid breaks them down into a sort of soup that the plant soaks up. Big pitcher plants can even attract and digest mice, frogs, and lizards!

FAST FACT

Some pitchers are so big they can drown a rat!

DID YOU KNOW?
A lid keeps rain from filling the pitcher. This would make the pitcher so heavy that it would break off the leaf.

lid

pitcher

Sundew

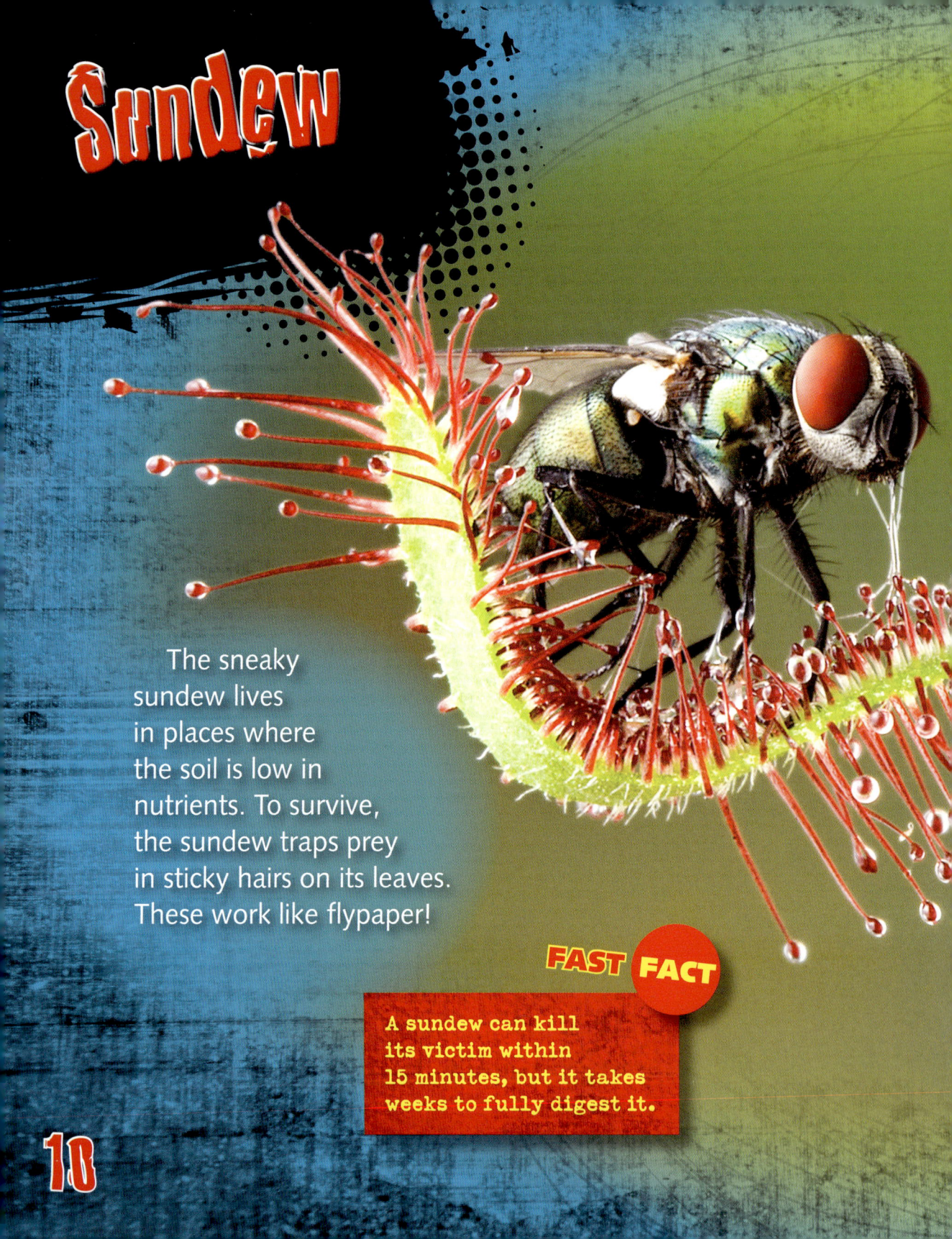

The sneaky sundew lives in places where the soil is low in nutrients. To survive, the sundew traps prey in sticky hairs on its leaves. These work like flypaper!

FAST FACT

A sundew can kill its victim within 15 minutes, but it takes weeks to fully digest it.

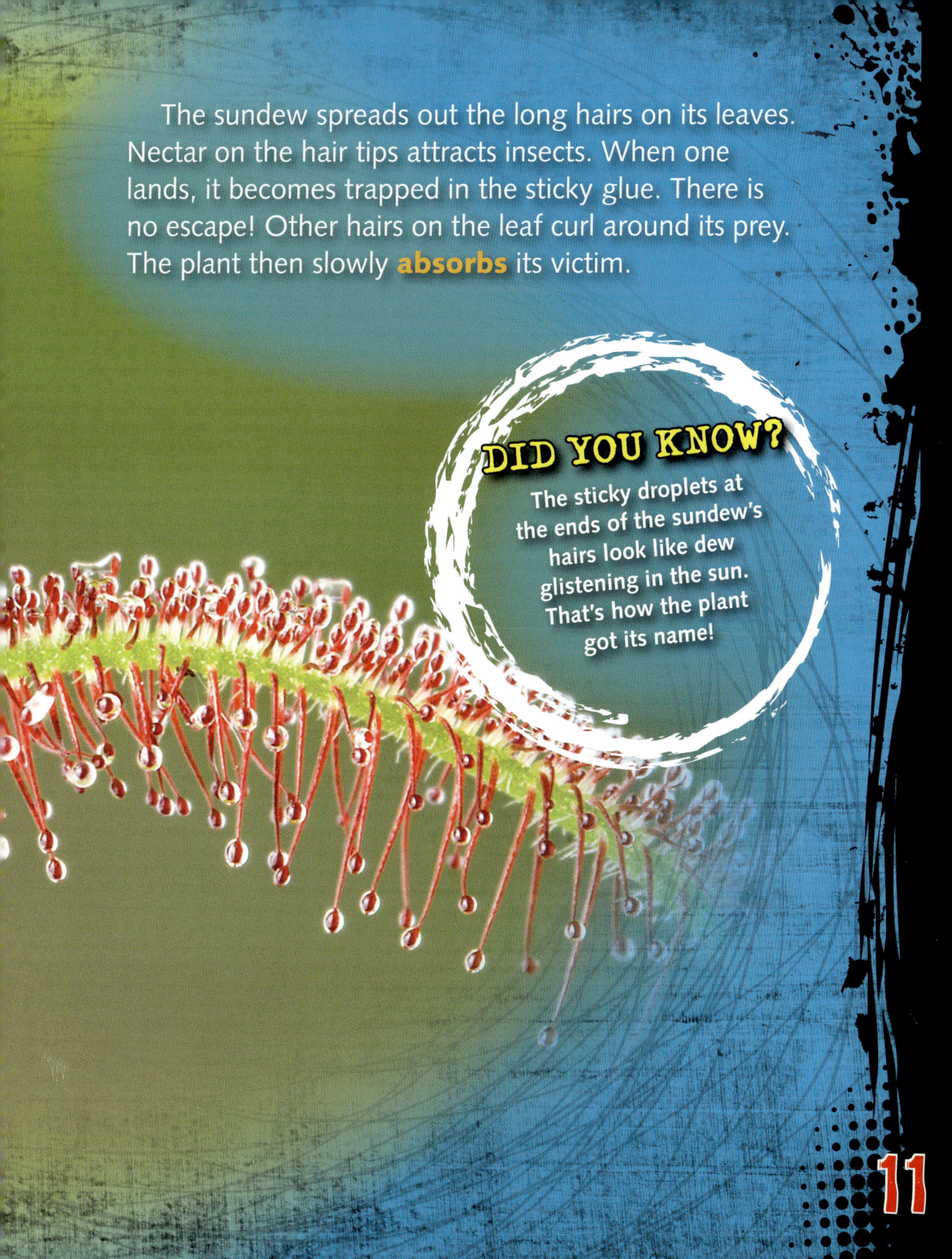

The sundew spreads out the long hairs on its leaves. Nectar on the hair tips attracts insects. When one lands, it becomes trapped in the sticky glue. There is no escape! Other hairs on the leaf curl around its prey. The plant then slowly **absorbs** its victim.

DID YOU KNOW?

The sticky droplets at the ends of the sundew's hairs look like dew glistening in the sun. That's how the plant got its name!

Bladderwort

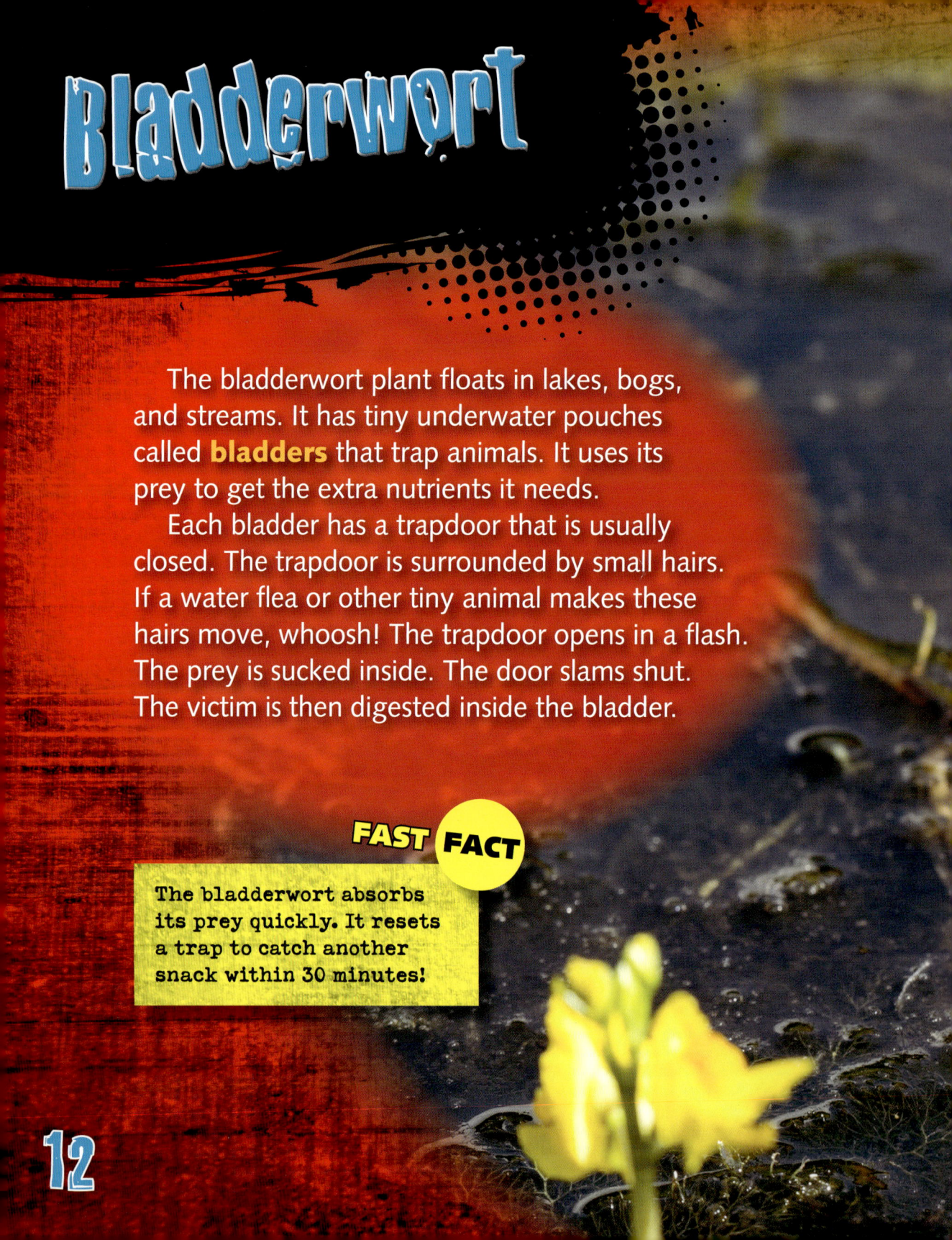

The bladderwort plant floats in lakes, bogs, and streams. It has tiny underwater pouches called **bladders** that trap animals. It uses its prey to get the extra nutrients it needs.

Each bladder has a trapdoor that is usually closed. The trapdoor is surrounded by small hairs. If a water flea or other tiny animal makes these hairs move, whoosh! The trapdoor opens in a flash. The prey is sucked inside. The door slams shut. The victim is then digested inside the bladder.

FAST FACT

The bladderwort absorbs its prey quickly. It resets a trap to catch another snack within 30 minutes!

bladder

DID YOU KNOW?

Bladderworts are one of the fastest plants in the world. Their bladders open and close so quickly people cannot see it happen!

Corkscrew Plant

Above ground, the corkscrew plant's cluster of leaves looks innocent. But beneath the soil, its long white leaves are a death trap! These special leaves have spiral tubes running through them. Each tube is lined with hairs that point inward.

DID YOU KNOW?

Corkscrew plants trap tiny animals that can only be seen with a microscope!

FAST FACT

The plant's trapping leaves grow up to 6 inches (15 centimeters) long.

Tiny animals crawl into the tubes. Once inside, there is no escape. The hairs allow the prey to travel farther in, but not back out. The animals are forced into a hollow chamber. There, digestive juices break down the prey. Then the plant absorbs its meal.

ACTIVITY

Engineering in Practice

Make a trap that uses inward pointing "hairs"!

- Roll a flat slab of modeling clay.
- Cut two straws into three pieces each.
- Stick the pieces into the clay in a row, but at a low angle.
- Lay your hand flat on one end of the clay and push it gently toward the straw "hairs." In one direction, your hand should glide over the hairs. In the opposite direction, it will be hard to escape!

Dodder

The dodder is a deadly **parasite**. It cannot make its own food. Its **seeds** grow in shallow soil. To survive, it must latch on to other plants. It steals nutrients from inside their bodies. The dodder has no leaves. Its thin orange **stems** look like spaghetti.

The stems grow upward by winding tightly around other plants. Little bumps on the sides of the stems invade the other plants. They then suck out nutrients from inside their victims. This attack can be **fatal** to its prey.

FAST FACT

The dodder curls around its prey counterclockwise. No one is sure why!

DID YOU KNOW?

Some dodder plants can make more than 16,000 seeds. These seeds can survive for up to 50 years in the soil!

Strangler Fig

Strangler figs live up to their gruesome name. They strangle other plants! A strangler fig starts growing on the branch of a tree. Over time, its long **roots** coil down and around the tree and into the ground.

The roots take in water and nutrients from the soil. They grow thicker and thicker. They grip the tree tighter and tighter. This keeps the tree from taking in water and nutrients for itself. The tree slowly dies, and the strangler fig takes its place.

FAST FACT

Strangler fig seeds are carried high into trees in the droppings of animals that eat the plant's fruit!

ACTIVITY

Engineering in Practice

Trees have tubes inside their trunks. These tubes carry water and nutrients up from the soil. Make this model to see how strangler figs kill trees!

- Stuff a cardboard tube with long straws. Try sucking up water through the straws.
- Attach some strings to the top of the tube so they hang down the sides.
- Now, wrap the strings around the tube and pull them tight.
- What happens to the straws inside? Can they still suck up water?

DID YOU KNOW?

The strangler fig grows wide roots. These keep it from falling over once it has killed its victim.

Puya

A prickly puya has a deadly secret. Its spiky leaves work like a barbed wire fence. They keep large animals from eating the flowers in the center of the plant.

FAST FACT

Animals as big as sheep have been victims of the puya's sharp spikes!

Animals avoid the plant because the spikes are sharp and hard as daggers. If an animal gets caught on the spikes, it cannot escape. It slowly starves to death. Its corpse rots in the ground nearby. Nutrients from the animal's body wash into the soil. These help the puya grow!

DID YOU KNOW?

Small birds squeeze between the puya's spikes to feed on nectar. The birds then help spread pollen from one puya to another.

Angel's Trumpet

Angel's trumpet is named for its trumpet-shaped flowers. These colorful blossoms hang upside-down like bells. But beware, this plant is a dangerous beauty!

All parts of the angel's trumpet are deadly. The seeds hold the most poison. Just touching the plant or breathing its scent can be painful.

DID YOU KNOW?

Some butterflies can eat angel's trumpet. They are not affected by the poison, which they store in their own bodies. This keeps animals from eating them, too!

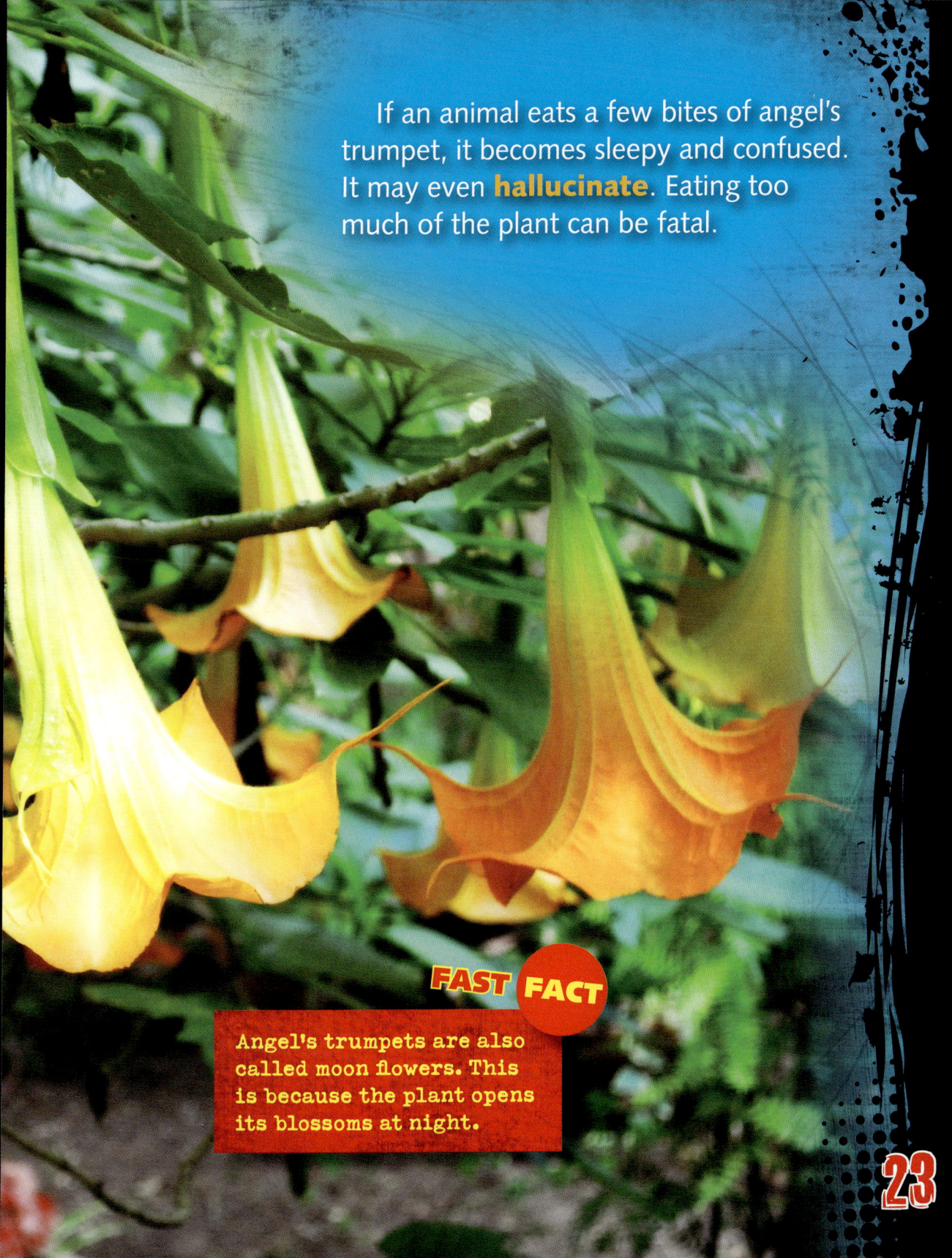

If an animal eats a few bites of angel's trumpet, it becomes sleepy and confused. It may even **hallucinate**. Eating too much of the plant can be fatal.

FAST FACT

Angel's trumpets are also called moon flowers. This is because the plant opens its blossoms at night.

Manchineel Tree

With its towering branches and small green fruits, the manchineel tree looks welcoming. But do not be fooled. The manchineel is the world's most dangerous tree!

All parts of the manchineel are poisonous. The tree oozes deadly white **sap** that burns the skin and leaves painful blisters. If the sap gets into a person's eyes, it can temporarily blind them.

Eating the tree's poisonous fruit makes a person's body feel like it is on fire. Even a single bite can be deadly!

DID YOU KNOW?

In the past, native people used the tree's sap to poison the tips of their arrows!

FAST FACT

In Spanish, the manchineel fruit is called *manzanilla de la muerte*. This means "little apple of death."

manchineel fruit

Doll's Eyes

The creepy doll's eyes plant looks like it is watching you! This plant grows shiny white berries on top of blood-red stems. The berries have small dark spots on the ends. They look like beady eyes!

DID YOU KNOW?

When birds eat the doll's eyes berries, its poison does not harm them. The birds later pass the seeds as waste. Then the seeds grow into new plants.

FAST FACT

The doll's eyes grows best in shady places. In a woodland, its "eyes" stand out in the gloom!

These bitter berries contain deadly poison. Eating more than five or six berries can be fatal. If an animal eats them, its heart stops. But most animals leave the plant alone anyway because the berries taste so bad!

Engineered to Survive

Some plants live in places where the soil is poor. They trap insects and other animals to survive. They get the nutrients from their prey they need to live and grow.

DID YOU KNOW?
Some poisonous plants have bright-red berries. This color warns animals to stay away!

Some plants strangle other plants to get the support they need to grow. Some invade other plants to steal their food. Others stab, sting, or poison animals to keep them away. Many of these plants also taste bad. This warns animals not to eat them. Nature designed these killer plants to survive.

FAST FACT

Holly has hard, spiky leaves that poke animals that try to eat the plant.

Glossary

absorbs—soaks up

adapt—to change to be better suited to a place

bladders—inflated, hollow sacs

digests—breaks down food for the body to use

engineered—designed and built

fatal—deadly

hallucinate—to see something that is not actually there

lures—draws in

nectar—the sugary substance found in flowers

nutrients—substances living things need to live and grow

parasite—a plant or animal that lives and feeds off another living thing and harms it

photosynthesis—the process by which plants make their own food from sunlight and air

poison—to give off a substance that can make animals sick or kill them

prey—animals that get hunted and eaten

roots—plant parts that grow underground; roots take in water and nutrients from soil.

sap—a fluid that carries food and water through a plant

seeds—the parts of plants that can grow into new plants

species—a specific kind of living thing

stems—the parts of plants that hold them upright and support their flowers and leaves

To Learn More

AT THE LIBRARY

Claybourne, Anna. *Killer Plants and Other Green Gunk.* New York, N.Y.: Crabtree Publishing Company, 2014.

Jones, Keisha. *Plants That Eat.* New York, N.Y.: PowerKids Press, 2016.

Owen, Ruth. *How Do Plants Defend Themselves?* New York, N.Y.: PowerKids Press, 2014.

ON THE WEB

Learning more about killer plants is as easy as 1, 2, 3.

1. Go to www.factsurfer.com.
2. Enter "killer plants" into the search box.
3. Click the "Surf" button and you will see a list of related websites.

With factsurfer.com, finding more information is just a click away.

Index

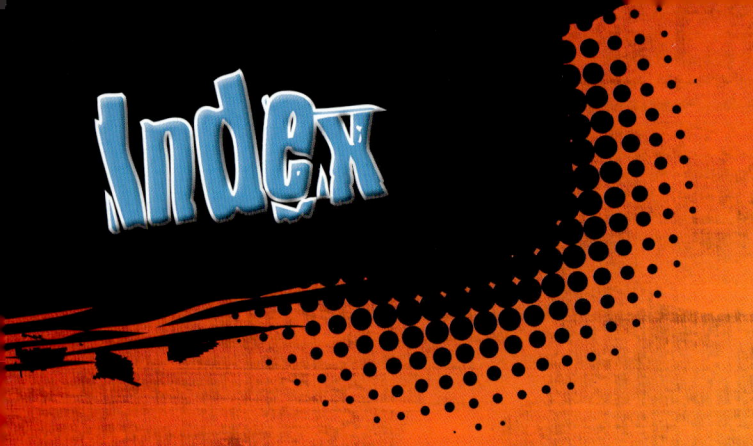

angel's trumpets, 22–23
berries, 26, 27, 28
bladderworts, 12–13
corkscrew plants, 14–15
dodders, 16–17
doll's eyes, 26–27
Engineering in Practice, 7, 15, 19
flowers, 20, 22, 23
fruit, 18, 24, 25
hairs, 6, 10, 11, 12, 14, 15
holly, 29
insects, 5, 6, 8, 11, 28
leaves, 6, 7, 9, 10, 11, 14, 15, 20, 29
manchineel trees, 24–25

nectar, 6, 8, 11, 21
nutrients, 5, 6, 10, 12, 16, 18, 19, 21, 28
parasite, 16
pitcher plants, 8–9
poison, 4, 5, 22, 24, 26, 27, 28, 29
puya plants, 20–21
seeds, 16, 17, 18, 22, 26
spikes, 6, 20, 21, 29
strangler figs, 18–19
sundews, 10–11
Venus flytraps, 6–7
water hemlock, 4, 5

The images in this book are reproduced through the courtesy of: Marco Uliana/ Shutterstock, front cover, pp. 1, 6–7; Andrew Park/ Shutterstock, pp. 4–5; Nature's Images/ Science Photo Library, pp. 8–9; Ling Kuok Loung/ Shutterstock, p. 9 (right); Cathy Keifer/ Shutterstock, pp. 10–11; Chris Moody/ Shutterstock, pp. 12–13; BMJ/ Shutterstock, p. 13 (top right); NoahElhardt/ Wikipedia, p. 14 (bottom); Rost'a Kracík/ Wikipedia, pp. 14–15; Dr. Morley Read/ Shutterstock, pp. 16–17; Jason Patrick Ross/ Shutterstock, p. 17 (top); Tor Pur/ Shutterstock, pp. 18–19; Lakov Filimonov/ Shutterstock, pp. 20–21; Lazaregagnidze/ Wikipedia, pp. 22–23; Darryl Brooks/ Dreamstime, pp. 24–25; Hans Hillewaert/ Wikipedia, p. 25 (bottom); Alex Polo/ Shutterstock, pp. 26–27; Kerioak - Christine Nichols/ Shutterstock, pp. 28–29.